THROUGH THE RIGHT EYE OF A TIGER

THROUGH THE RIGHT EYE OF A TIGER

WITH MY FINGER ON THE TRIGGER

LEO J VAILLANCOURT

authorHOUSE®

AuthorHouse™
1663 Liberty Drive
Bloomington, IN 47403
www.authorhouse.com
Phone: 1-800-839-8640

Published by AuthorHouse   03/27/2013

ISBN: 978-1-4772-6702-8 (sc)
ISBN: 978-1-4772-6701-1 (e)

Library of Congress Control Number: 2012916411

LEO J VAILLANCOURT KOREA 1950-1951

This is a story about Leo J. Vaillancourt's tour of duty during the Korean War from 1950 to 1951. He enlisted into the U.S. Army September 1948, completing 20 years of service, and then, retiring from the U.S. Army June 1969.

As a tank gunner on a M46 Tank, much of the story is what was observed through a gunner's periscope and the 6 power telescopic sight used for sighting the 90 mm gun.

The right eye of a tiger is explained in the story. All of the events in this story took place before I was 21 years of age, and had an influence on me the remainder of my life. This is by no means the only event that took place while I was in Korea, but only what I can recall.

More than 60 years have passed; I owe my life to the Offices and NCO's of my unit. We completed all assigned missions and they kept unit casualties down, because of their knowledge and leadership. Most of them had WW2 experience.

THROUGH
THE
RIGHT EYE
OF
A TIGER

With my finger on the trigger . . .
July 3, 2011

THROUGH THE EYES OF A TIGER

LEO VAILLANCOURT KOREA
1950-1951

ALERT

I enlisted in the army September 1948 and received

my basic training at Fort Dix NJ. After basic training

I was sent to a leader's course at Fort Dix. When

the Korean War broke out in June 1950, I was a

20-year-old privet first class, stationed at Fort Hood

Texas (Home of the Second Armored Division) in

a peace time Army. After five months of playing

football for Fort Hood, 2nd Armored Division I

worked as DS (detach service) at Fort Hood Leaders

Course as an assistance instructor. I did odd jobs at the school for about 4 or 5 months before the war.

My parent duty station was A Company 66 Medium Tank Battalion, 2nd Armored Division. A few days after the Korean War started I was instructed to report back to my unit. After reporting to my 1st Sergeant, he said, "Don't unpack your bags you have been transferred to A company 6 med Tank Battalion across the street."

I walked across the street, and reported to the First Sergeant. He instructed me to report to the battalion personal. There I had my records check, and then told to report to the Medics at the dispensary, where I received an update of all my shots. In addition, I was then told to go to the dental clinic, at which time I had two teeth filled. That night I was paid up-to-date, received new field gear, and was told to call home—up at 3AM.

The unit was loaded onto a troop train, Destination—Camp Stoneham Cal. The next day we loaded on a troop ship, and we were on our way to Korea. The troop ship was made to hold 1800 troops; we loaded with 2400 troops abroad. The Army can move real fast when it needs too.

TROOP SHIP

A Troop Ship is to carry troops, equipment, and cargo to the war zone. Some of the ship compartments had to sleep in shifts because of the number of troops aboard.

We had a 10 day trip ahead of us. It was stormy weather the first three days, and the seas were choppy—many became sea sick. However, I did not.

With bunks four tiers high, and equipment with duffel bags everywhere, there was not much room to move around. Many men played cards to pass the time.

They did have an outside movie one night. It was a slap stick movie.

When the bad weather ended, my buddy and I found a life raft to sleep in on deck. It smelt much better up on deck. Ordinarily they would be off limits to everyone—emergency use only. I guess this was an emergency.

During the day it was so overcrowded on deck, it was difficult to find a place at the rail to gaze at the water and watch fish jump. The water was as smooth as glass, most of the time. It was very hot; the showers were cold salt water.

Soap would not suds up in salt water; it would turn to a sticky paste. We had fun trying to get the paste off our body.

In a few days salt water soap was issued to wash with, this worked much better.

We did not talk much about the war. A class was given about Korea and its people. The ship did put out a ship newspaper telling us what was going on in Korea and at home. Not much news, just some.

I did not see one ship or airplane pass us by. The food was not bad. We spent much of our time in the long chow line. We had to eat standing. They did have a ship canteen where candy and cigarettes were sold.

ARRIVING TO THE WAR (KOREA)

One morning a mountain top broke through the clouds—It was Mount Fuji. We were in Japan! The top of the mountain came into sight before land was spotted. Tug boats towed the troop ship into the harbor. We no sooner got tides up to the dock when the ship got a change of orders—go to Korea ASAP.

It took the rest of the day and night. When we approached Korea early in the morning, August 6,

1950, I could hear artillery and sometimes see the tracers of 50 Cal machine guns. Some units went straight to the front line. We had to wait for our tanks, which would be arriving on other cargo ships.

It took a few days to receive our new M46 Tanks we had to prepare the tank for combat. We had to check and load the tank with ammo and get the equipment ready.

I found out later we were the first full combat units to arrive by ship from the United States as reinforcements. Small support units and troop causality replacements came by air transport.

INTRODUCTION TO THE
M46 PATTON TANK

The M46 Patton Tank was field tested at Fort Hood by the 6th Tank Bn. Top brass thought this was a good time to combat test the M46 Tank. I did all my tank training on the M4 Sherman Tank (used during WW2) at Fort Hood and assigned as a gunner on my new M46 tank. I never fired a 90mm gun.

I spent about one hour with my platoon leader in the turret. He introduced me to the M46 turret and showed me everything once. I had to know about the 90mm gun, ammunition, gun sights, and turret controls.

There was not too much difference in comparison to M4 Sherman Tank. The Sherman tank had 76 mm gun and a gyro stabilizer for firing on the move, and the M46 Patton tank did not.

A VISIT FROM AN INFANTARY SARGEANT

As I was working on my tank, an infantry sergeant from the 19th Regiment 24th Inf. Div., came up to me and asked for a new 30cal machine gun barrel. He said his 30cal was completely worn out and that the Nag-tong River had turned red with North Korean blood as they tried to take Pusan. Also, he said they had to move the machine gun for field of fire because bodies piled up in front of the machine gun. That's when his gun barrel burned out.

Equipment was hard to get. He had been in Korea from the start of the war. This was the first time they were off line since the war started, to resupply and regroup.

I had two extra barrels, so I gave him one. We soon went on line with the 19th Infantry.

GOING TO THE WAR FRONT

The first thing I noticed while moving to the front was all the wounded returning from the front lines—mostly South Korean troops. We moved along the front line to booster the line where needed.

One day, we crossed the Nantong River fording the river to cross it. The M46 tank can ford about 4 feet of water. The engineers were building a pontoon bridge for equipment and supplies to cross. We were to set up on the other side of the river so the engineers could work on the bridge all night. I had first guard.

My company set up a perimeter and I took a 30cal Machine Gun from my tank. I took it down a trail next to the river. I was to give an early warning for the company. I was only about an hour into my 2 hour shift, I was behind my Machine Gun, and all was quiet except for the engineers working. A dog came running up the trail. When he saw me he stopped, he turned and ran back down the trail. Then, I saw a man's head, then two silhouetted against the river. I opened fire!

All hell broke loose. Most of the tanks behind me opened up returning fire. With all that fire power we didn't have any more trouble that night. They finished the bridge during the night.

AMBUSH

The next day we received orders to move up the road a few miles. A tank Company would stretch out about one mile on a road and march with 17 tanks, maintenance trucks, a tank retriever, and supply and kitchen trucks.

During the road march my tank had to stop. This was because our throttle linkage came apart on my tank and we had to fix it. The unit also stopped. It was time for a pit stop anyway. We pulled over and fixed the linkage. We made repairs quickly.

As we were moving up to the unit, we notice a company of (150) North Korean soldiers coming off the hill behind my unit. They thought they were going to attack my stopped unit from the rear. Many Armored units have been ambushed while stopped on the road. Many of our troops were on the ground checking over the tank tracks, oil levels, etc., so we stopped, and reported what we saw to the company commander over the radio. The enemy still did not see us!

He alerted the unit for action. Then, he instructed my tank to fire the 90mm behind them so they would not return from where they came from. As the gunner, I opened fire up the hill using the 90mm and 30cal guns. The tank commander used the 50cal forcing the enemy to come down the hill and into an open rice paddy. The unit had a field day, with enemy troops in the open. Not many, if any, got away.

When the smoke lifted, we moved on to our next support mission. My unit moved up on line to support the infantry. My tank was deployed on a hill. We didn't go to the top, but just before the crest as to not silhouette the tank on the skyline during daylight hours. We would top the hill at night so we would have fields of fire.

The tank commander and I went up to the crest to see what the terrain was like on the other side. The purpose of this was to make a range card to be used during night firing.

When I saw an Infantry man sitting on a rock eating c rations I heard gun fire coming from a hill across a valley about 800 yards out. I saw dirt kick up a few yards from him, so I shouted to him to let him know he was being shot at!

He calmly said "I know. He has been doing it for about an hour. He can't hit shit."

Later that day, three men was to go to the front slope of the hill to dig to place a machine gun for a listening post for the night. It was hot, so one of them went for more water, and the other man came back for something also. While the third man was digging the emplacements alone, he was jumped by 4 North Koreans. (They thought they would take him prisoner.)

We heard screaming down the hill. When help got to him they found he had killed three of them with his entrenching tool, a small shovel all troops carried, and was on top of the other man with his hands around his throat screaming. Being taken as a prisoner was something I had a hard time with. I don't think I could accept being taken as a prisoner.

USO SHOW

One day we were back with the artillery when we were asked if anybody would want to see a USO show—one would be here within the hour. A few of us went to see them, and were very excited. We never had any shows come to us before. This was the first one! It was some Western outfit.

We sat on the side of a hill and watched them set up. They had a big trailer that opened into a stage. One incoming artillery shell exploded in the area as soon as the show was about to begin. They panicked, folded their stage, and were gone faster than it took to say it. We all just sat there and watched them go.

When they were out of sight, we returned to our unit.

I never saw a USO show in Korea. Only rear area troops got to see them.

SEPTEMBER 1950 (BAPTISM OF FIRE)

My unit was to spear head a move to Songju, supporting the 21th Infantry, Regiment 24th Infantry Division. We moved all night, stopping before entering the city.

When daylight came, the infantry moved out ahead of us in double files—one on each side of to the road.

As soon as they started to move artillery and motor fire, it started to rain in. I saw a round had exploded nearby, picking up 3 infantry men off their feet, blowing them into the air. Receiving order for the tanks to take the lead in the attack, we moved up fast and took the lead. As we did the artillery continued;

we came around a big hill on our right, rice paddy on the left, and a small village straight ahead.

As my tank was leading the column, I started to fire my 30 caliber machine gun into the village. My tank commander gave me the order "ante tank gun to the left." I whipped the turret to the left searching the terrain for targets, the loader thru a round of HE (high explosives) into the chamber of the 90MM gun, all the while smoke was coming into the turret from shells exploding on the outside of the tank. I saw smoke and flash coming from across a rice paddy.

As the cross hairs of my site came across the target I squeezed the trigger of my firing mechanism firing the 90mm. I fired 4 rounds, then the tank commander commanded "antitank gun to the font" I whipped the turret to the front, and again I saw flashes and smoke from AT (antitank Gun) guns going off. I fired

3 more rounds of HE (High Explosive) at the enemy in-placement about 50 yards away. My tank did not stop moving forward. Shells were still exploding outside the tank. There was alot of smoke and noise.

Then the tank commander ordered the driver to "stop and back up!" As we were about to overrun the position, he did as he was ordered. I heard him over the intercom say, "turn this tank around." As the driver tried to comply with the order both tracks came off the tank.

Most of the road wheels had been blown off the tank, placing us in a rice paddy facing the left. I thought to myself: no tracks; we are now a pill box. The tank began to sink into the rice paddy mud. I tried to elevate the gun so as to bring fire on the guns in front of me. The gun was stuck. I kept trying, but all I could see from my sights was water. I fired one round of 90mm to see if I could free it—no luck.

The tank commander then ordered to abandon tank. If I stay here I will get it, if I go out I will get it. I will take my chance outside.

The tank commander had left the turret. On the way out I picked up three hand grenades from the grenade box. I stood on top of the turret looked around to see what my next move would be as two round exploited alongside of the tank. I don't know if I jumped or got blown off the tank, I found myself in the rice paddy in about 1 foot of water. I crawled to the left of the tank to a knoll about 50 yards away. I lost my wrist watch in the move. I found a wagon and crawled under it. It had corn storks staked against it.

The driver came running over to where I was. I shouted for him to get down. Small arms fire was splashing water around him as he was running.

He got down and crawled next to me under the wagon.

The next thing I knew the air force appeared and begin strafing the area. Then they dropped napalm. (Jelly gas bomb) They were so close I could feel the heat from the flame. F51 came firing all guns. They were about 50 to 100 feet off the ground. 50 cal brass and links were falling around us as they flew over. When it all quitted down we got up and looked around. I looked into the wagon we were under. It was filled with 120 mm artillery rounds. God was with us! The enemy fled area for the nearby hills. They have enough.

The North Korean unit had enough and had fled the area. The tank behind us ran over a mine and blew a track blocking the road. I said "let's find the rest of the crew." The tank engine was still running as I ran to the tank and switched it off. We found the rest of the crew across the road in a ditch.

The tank commander had been wounded, but the rest of us were okay. I counted six holes in his back. We dressed the wounds the best we could. I went back to the tank to call for medical help. I was told they could not send the medics because the road was mined, so I got the rammer staff from the tank and with blankets made a stretcher to carry our tank commander out of the area to the medics.

The unit left us behind to make repairs on the tank as they moved on. We took parts from the tank that ran over the anti-tank mine and in a few days all repairs were made. I found we were hit 15 times by anti-tank guns, the tank received Road wheels, allot of track and outside damage with no penetrations, I have credit for 5 guns kill. I fired 8 rounds of high explosive. We found 12 ante tank guns in the area. Most guns were less than 100 yards from us. We found out later our tank commander received the Silver Star. I was made a sergeant. At the time of the battle a liaison plane was over head and saw the battle. A reporter was with them and sent a report to the news or time magazine. The name of the article was *Love that Bounce.*

REJOINING THE UNIT

Our tank caught up and rejoined our unit at Taejon. When we arrived the North Korean army had been forced out of the area. I saw some women and children crying and digging with their bare hands in the ground behind a church. I found out later that the South Korean men that would not go with the retreating North Korean army, they were made to dig their graves and then buried alive. This was about the same time other units made the landing at Inchon.

As my unit moved north in South Korea toward North Korea, we found large mounds of dirt on the outskirt of many villages, with the whole village have been killed by retreating North Koreans army—North Koreans are not nice people.

HOME FOR CHRISTMAS

There was talk of going home for Christmas. We spear headed all the way thru West side of North Korea.

It was starting to get cold now, and had to get a new tank, we many miles on the old one. It was showing its age—rubber pads on the tracks worn to the steel bars. And sprockets were worn badly and missing fenders. I was on my 3rd Tank when I left Korea.

TANK BATTLE

One day as we were spearheading a move, while on a mountain road, my unit was fired app-on by Russian made T34 tanks from the Valley below. They had us one behind the other—No place to go! Our lead tank was hit by the first rounds fired and had its track blown off. This blocked the road, and we could not back up. The entire 24th Infantry Division was behind us. We fired at their flashes of gun fire.

One by one we knocked out the tanks on the valley below. One of our tanks lost a track, another lost a muffler. Another tank lost some baggage from the outside. The enemy lost four tanks and some AT guns. They did not know what they were doing. The enemy was using HE (high explosives) instead of AP (armor parsing) ammo. This was a no contest!

We did have a hard time getting the Infantry off our tanks so we could fight properly. Infantry often ride on the outside of our tanks so, they didn't have to walk or ride in trucks—no PC (personnel carrier) for infantry at that time. The unit and column moved on to the next fire fight.

THANKSGIVING DAY 1950

Thanksgiving Day 1950 we moved to the north all day. It was starting to get real cold now; we were near the Manchurian border west side of Korea. I heard about the Chinese but had no contact with them.

The 24th Inf. Div. was going after the last strong hold of the North Korean army. It was now time to stop and resupply with gas and ammo, and check over the tank before the last big push.

We had a turkey sandwich that was cooked on moving trucks. The unit then gassed up received c rations for the next day meal. We made last checks of equipment; my unit linked with the infantry, and then moved out.

Now dark, we received a large amount of small arms fire from across the river. To minimize casualty a decision was made to wait until morning before moving on in the city of Pack chon.

In the morning we found most the enemy had moved on during the night. Our lead tank reported tank tracks moving out of town. Captain Jack Moss our CO told the tank commander to track it down and clobber him. The tank was found later that day, and it was a banded. They had no heart for a fight.

ENEMY AIR

As we moved forward I heard over the tank command channel, that enemy air was strafing the rear of the column. The tank column stopped. All was quiet. I turn around and found I was alone in the tank. I stuck my head out of the tank turret to see what was going on, and saw a Russian yak, a fighter plane, all aflame as it pass over my head about 200 feet above the tank and crashed in the trees not much farther away. I heard later our air force took them out in a Arial combat dog fight.

The attack Column continues the march towards the Chinese border. The column tank was moving so fast we were ordered to slow down so the infantry could keep up with us. Who were riding in the trucks?

We were now in what was later called Mig Alley, (This area is where the Russian Mig 15 had aerial dog fights with U.S. F86 Saber Jet) The unit moved forward and set up positions before dark before entering the city of Sinuiju, on the river and Manchurian border.

A Chinese patrol found us that night about 9PM. The same time we got orders to pull back. The North Korean Army is no longer a fighting force. UN Forces have taken the North Korean Army out. The Chinese Army was now on the move and into the war. All units have been hit and most units have been over run. The Chinese are now in the war.

No survivors on that Chinese patrol, they didn't know what hit them. We waited for them to get up close to us, The Infantry tried to capture them, but we took them by surprise as they started to run in all directions.

The infantry cut them down.

REAR GUARD

We pulled back a few miles and had to wait for our gas trucks. Every unit was pulling back but us. We got the job of rear guard, along with a Company of Infantry.

Units to our right were getting hit very hard; we had encountered only light enemy patrols. It was getting real cold. Our units did not receive any cold weather gear.

Everybody thought we would be on our way home when the North Korean Army was gone. Our gas trucks arrived just before daylight and we pulled back.

A few days later we received orders to go on the offensive. As did the Chinese Army did the same.

All UN units were again overrun by over whelming numbers of Chinese troops.

VERY COLD NIGHT

My unit again had the mission of rear guard. Yet again, we had to wait for gas supply to catch up. Tanks burn 3 gallons a mile.

One night we had an infantry company with us, as we moved into a village. From what we could tell the village was empty—no civilians.

I heard an Infantry Sargent tell four men from his squad to go up on a knoll for a listening post for the night.

Instructions were to return to the unit at daylight because we would be moving as soon as the tanks got gassed up.

That night it was very cold with high winds. It was so cold—with parsing winds that penetrated to the bone.

The only way to get any warmth was to get into your sleeping bag. I still got chilled!

The next morning as we were getting ready to move out the four men had yet to return. I heard the Infantry Sergeant tell two men to go up after them.

A few minutes later the two men returned and said "They're not coming down Sergeant".

He asked "Why not".

The soldier replied, "They are all dead. They froze to death last night."

This was not an uncommon event.

One night an Infantry man came up to me and asked for a blanket for the night. He was shaking all over; hypothermia was already setting in. I asked what happened to his equipment. He said his unit had been over run the other night and he lost all his equipment.

Supply has not caught up with them yet. So I let him have a poncho and a blanket for the night. I told him if he was with me the next night he could have it again. In the morning he returned my equipment. I did not see him again.

NIGHT TROOP REPLACEMENT

One night an Infantry unit we were with was getting replacement troops. It was very dark that night, no moon, over cast, and real dark. The unit received 18 new men about 1 AM.

By 5 AM the Chinese Army attacked the unit and over ran them. The unit had to pull back off the hill. During the battle our Infantry lost 20 men—15 of them were the new replacements just received.

The Commander said, "That is the last time I will send new troops on the line at night."

COLD, COLD, VERY COLD

The weather was very cold—your face, hands, and feet were always cold. You tried to heat your c ration by lighting a small fire, or use the muffler of your vehicle for a heater. The outer edge would be burned, but the center was always a small ball of ice.

There were no heaters in the M46 tank. At times I envied the Infantry because they could walk to keep warm; I had to stay in my tank with cold steel all around me not being able to move around. The tank turret was like the inside of a freezer.

To get warm, sometimes someone would find an old tire, put gas and oil in it and set it on fire. We had no wood or trees to burn. I got so dirty; I knew I would never ever get clean again.

I always slept outside next to my tank on the ground. I did this rain or snow. When I slept in my sleeping bag I would put a round in the chamber of my 45 pistol corked and locked.

Many men were caught in their sleeping bags at night during an enemy attack. I would place my boots under my head for a pillow. When putting my boots back on I would have to scrape the frost from the inside of each boot with my bare hands before putting them on. I would have to stop and warm my hands for each boot. It was always so cold! It was so cold my Ansco Camera froze on me.

I bent the shutter handle trying to take a photo. It froze up on me. I have no cold weather photos of Korea. I put my camera into my bag until spring.

TRYING TO GET CLEAN

We always stayed either on the front lines, or on the move. Showers were something I dreamed about. No shower units in forward positions.

Our steel helmets were used to heat water to bath with, and try to stay clean. I recall a day when Four Austrian's asked me if they could borrow an axe from my tank. They went to a nearby river, chopped a hole in the ice, jumped in, and took a bath in ice water. Keeping clean was a problem.

THE CHILDREN

One thing I never could get use to was when we were near a village, and it was time to eat, the children would come out and stare at you eating. God only knows when they had their last meal. I would end up giving most of my meal away. At times I would have to hide to eat. It tears my heart out to see the children so hungry all the time.

Women would go into the garbage can to get food for their children. It was so sad to see this as a young man. And we thought we had it bad growing up.

REFUGEES

You could always tell when an attack was imminent. All you had to do was watch the civilians in the surrounding area.

When they all start moving south, you knew something was about to happen—soon. I recall one very cold night all the civilians were on the move. The line of people must have been several miles long, having travelled from little villages just off the main road and from back in the hills. They had all their belongings in small carts, on their backs, and on their heads.

Small children, old people, some sick or too old to walk would be strapped in chairs. The chairs were strapped on the backs of the family members. I don't know how far they plan on going that night or how far they have traveled that day. But I am sure many of them did not make it thru that very cold night.

All they wanted to do was to get out of the way of the War. There was no way any of us could help them. The small kids—I felt sorry for them as they passed by us most of the night.

A few days later the Chinese were on the move again.

PROTECTING ARTILLERY UNITS

When the hills were too high for tanks to climb, we protected a flank of artillery units. At times the artillery would sound like machine gun fire. When this happens we knew the enemy was on the move.

When they found large enemies buildup of troops, artillery would fire (TOT) time on target. All available artillery units would participate in the fire mission.

I recall one such mission in the Kumar Valley. The infantry had the high ground to our front—my unit. A Company 6 Tank had the mission of guard duty around the artillery flank. The high ground ran north and south with a main road in the center. When the TOT started I could hear a roar like thunder from afar in our rear. 8" howitzers firing, then 155mm long toms joined in, and then 155mm howitzers a little closer, with the roar getting closer and closer. When the 105 howitzers joined in, it was like machine guns firing with more than a battalion of 105s firing at once. Then last was the *flut flut* of the infantry mortars. Then there was a big roar of the massive explosions hitting the ground all at once.

I surely would not like to be on the receiving end of this load. As I was gazing up into to sky I saw a L19 liaison air plane come around the hill very low, and exploded in midair. It must have run into an artillery round? I did not see anything fall from the sky. This L19 must have called in the strike.

Two days later the Chinese army was on the move again. Again we had to pull back. And again the armored units had to pull rear guard.

YEAR OF THE TIGER

The Year of 1950 was the Year of the Tiger. For the Chinese the story goes: if a person meets a tiger it would be bad luck for him. Someone in higher headquarters got the idea to paint tigers on all our tanks. This made our tanks look like tigers.

Teams of artist come from Higher HQ to do the job of painting the Tiger on all our tanks. We had instructions to place our tank on the high ground in plain sight, so everyone could see them. I am sure if they did meet up with one of our tanks it would be bad luck for them.

CHINESE DIGGING IN

In a defensive position at night in the early spring near the 38th parallel, I heard the Chinese from across the field digging in. They were making all sorts of noise: blowing bugles, shouting at each other, and blowing whistles. Maybe they were trying to make us nervous?

We thought they were about to attack. Then suddenly it got very quiet. I could make out someone crying, then someone shouting. Then it was quite again. Our Infantry mortar squad dropped mortars on them all that night.

When daylight came, I saw two Chinese soldiers walking toward us in the middle of the road. They have had enough, and gave up. They said it seemed every place they would go the same mortar squad was out to get them.

All our mortar squads received orders to fire the same paten of fire all the time. It looks like it worked. My unit did not take many prisoners. We would turn them over to the infantry.

CHINESE ARTILLERY

It was still very cold. As my unit was getting ready to occupy defensive positions, we were being observed by the Chinese Army. Artillery started to rain in on us. Our artillery was on the move to the rear at this time, with no return fire. Our air support was busy someplace else, with no place to take cover in an open field, we were in the open. We were somewhat bunched up, not spread out as we normally would be.

The order came over the radio "Hold your positions!"

About 30-40 rounds of 120mm came in. When the blast came close, we would move the tank so they had a hard time bracketing. The noise was as loud as I have ever heard as shells exploded just outside of the tank. I don't think it was that cold, but I was shaking all over. I was not the only one that was scared that day. I had nothing to do but just sit there in my gunner's seat.

The noise and smoke seem like it went on forever. I felt like a duck in a rain barrel. We soon got the order to move out of the area and took up new defense position. One tank had a track blown off. Our bedrolls and clothes strapped to the outside of the tanks had holes from shrapnel. Later I cut my hand as I was washing. I hadn't realized there was razor sharp shrapnel in my bar of soap!

CHINESE NIGHT ATTACK

One cold night in the Kumar valley, we were in a defensive position our tanks were spread out over a mile wide on the Kumar valley floor, with an infantry company dug in between the tanks. The night was cold, but not as cold that it has been, and the only noise was our own artillery firing a round or two every 5 or 10 minutes.

My tank was on flat ground with good field of fire. The tank commander was in the command hatch on 1st shift guard, the loader asleep on the turret floor, and the driver in his seat. I was too big with all the winter gear to relax in the gunner's seat, so I raped in a blanket and sat on the ground next to my tank, and slept for about an hour or so.

Waking up, I got a sudden notion to get in my tank. As I climbed onto the tank, I asked the tank commander how everything was.

He said, "Too quiet—only our own artillery going off."

I climbed down to the gunner's seat. I no sooner got there when I looked thru my periscope and saw our trip flares going off. Then I heard the Infantry shouting "here they come"! The driver cranked over the engine. I received the order to commence firing. Captain Moss (my CO) told us to turn on our head lights so we could see what we were shooting.

When the head lights came on, it looked like Fen Way Park. We had 15 tanks on line—each tank having a 90mm, 2 30cal machine guns and a 50 cal machine. With all guns firing, we did not even slow them down.

They told us later about 40'000 Chinese ran through us that night. All units online were over run.

Then the CO came over the radio and said in a clam voice, "It looks like we have been over run. Let's pull back. 1st platoon lead, 3rd, 2nd take up the rear. Move out. Watch your rear, move out. Follow me."

He was in his jeep. His driver told me later he was shooting them with his 45 as they were passing by while standing in the jeep.

I don't know what happened to the Infantry, they must have just taken off

Moving a good part of the night, we stopped next to a 105 artillery unit. They were firing with the guns pointing almost straight up.

When daylight came we pulled back. What a mess with all units mixed together.

Later that day we had to go back to help a unit that was cut off. When we got there the Chinese was waiting for us. They had blocked off the road, stopping the column. They then came down off the after us. They used explosives they held by hand against the tank until it exploded. The tank rocked with each explosion. We had to fire our machine guns at each other to help keep them off our tanks.

The bow gunner said over the intercom "Someone is pulling at my gun!"

I said, "Shoot him." I hit one Chinese in the head with my 90mm as I was power traversing the turret around. We pulled back with the trapped unit. I don't remember what else happened that day. It was a very long day.

ARMORED PATROL

One day my unit had a mission—to go on a combat daylight armored patrol behind enemy lines. We went about 4 or 5 miles behind the front line. Everything was going smooth until a tank from the second platoon ran over a mine and blew off a track.

We continued on blasting up the Chinese rear area. I saw a lone solder running with a full field pack on his back rifle at high port. My tank commander told me to take him out. I had the cross hairs on him; I reach to switch on the gun and fired. I switch on the main gun instead of the 30 cal machine gun by mistake. When the smoke cleared he had vanished. At this time the tank that ran over the mine was receiving mortar fire.

Preventing them from fixing the blown off track. The unit returned in short order. The company's (tank retriever) was on site to assist the crew in making repairs. Mortar was still coming in. As I scanned the top of the ridge line (with my 6 power telescope)

I noticed a small bush on the top of the hill that suddenly appeared. I told the loader to place a round of HE on delay. He did and I fired. The round hit the top of the hill; it bounced off and burst in the air. A nice air burst. All mortar fire stopped. The units returned home.

We had a nice hot corn beef hash for supper that night, fresh out of the can! Bread was also out of a can. It was like cake—really good.

AIRBORN DROP

My unit moved into Soul (the South Korean Capital) after the Chinese was pushed out by UN Forces. It was now early spring and the Communist forces were on the move north again.

On Good Friday,1951, my unit got the job to link up with the air born that dropped at Monson (about 40 miles north of Soul) They were to cut off the retreating North Korean Forces.

The road to Monson was heavily mined. We were to link up before dark. Several lead tanks had their tracks blown off. And a jeep went off the road and ran over a mine, killing two men.

We got the job to find a way around the mine field. We took to the shallow river bed nearby. My platoon leader walked in front of the lead tank most of the way in the river bed. He said he could see most of the mines. We were told to stay in line.

When we linked up with the Airborne it was dark, real dark—no moon. I went up on the hill to tell the Infantry where the tank would be for the rest of the night. Our airborne troops were all green troops first time in combat.

The next day more airborne troops dropped in by parachute with supplies. Every time an airplane would drop troops or supplies, the North Koreans would fire their artillery on the drop zone. The 6th Tank Battalion had a perimeter around the drop zone of 70 tanks.

An Artillery unit arrived and took the Korean artillery under fire. An artillery duel is something to see. One would fire, and then the other would return fire. The battle did not last too long—we won.

Later that day we moved on to yet another mission.

INFANTRY CLOSE SUPPORT

One day my unit had the mission of supporting Infantry as they were taking high ground to our front.

The hill was too steep for our tanks to climb being nearly 700 feet high.

We had good fields of fire. We watch an infantry squad go up the hill. As the squad leader lead his squad, we would fire in support. A tracer bullet would point to our next target. At times it looked like the support was too close to the advancing unit. As we gave him the support he asked for, he led his squad from one hole to and other.

The enemies were really dug in. This looked like a do or die effort on their part. The squad was just about to the top of the hill when a lone North Korean jumped out of an emplacement just a few yards from the squad leader and cut him down with a burp gun. Then he ran up the hill to another emplacement. Every tank had their eyes on him as we sent five 90mm rounds his way. I don't think he knew what hit him. The Infantry soon took the hill. Nobody felt good after this mission.

R & R

I never got to go on R & R to Japan. After serving in Korea for 6 months you were eligible to go to Japan for five days for rest and recreation. A few of my

buddies made it. They had some stories to tell when

they returned to the unit.

ORDERS FOR HOME

When I received my orders to return to the States,

I did not believe them at first. We had been pushed

back by the Chinese army and we had lost several

tanks in the company over the last few days. I didn't

think anybody was going any place? The only people

going home were the wounded.

I had a Russian rifle I had picked up some time ago.

I usually had it strapped on the outside of my tank

with the bags. I looked at it, and it had dust, dirt, mud

all over it. I knew it would take some time to clean

it properly. I asked if anybody wanted to have it. I

had no takers, so I broke the stork and threw it in

the dump. I had to return my pistol to supply before going to the airport.

GOING HOME

In Japan I started processing. We all had a steak dinner for our first meal Japan. Then was issued new class A-uniforms. I was sleeping in a room with about 50 other men also going home. The bunks were staked two high.

In the middle of the night someone had a nightmare and started shouting *HERE THEY COME—HERE THEY COME*. Some jumped out of bed and started to run and ran into the wall, some fell out of the top bunks onto the floor. Some trip over each other. Nobody owned up to who called the alarm. It's a good thing he may not have made it home.

I had another boat ride home. On the boat I had the job of being in charge of the KP's (kitchen police) in the mess hall. I got along good with the cooks. The job kept me busy, and time went by fast. The boat landed in Seattle Washington. I don't remember the exact date and time. I was home safe and sound.

In 10 ½ months in Korea, my unit, A Company 6th Med Tank Bn. 24th Inf. Div. had only 2 killed in action, with 50% wounded. Most walking wounded and nobody was captured by the enemy. Most of the Officers and NCOs were WW2 veterans. They knew their job, and did it.

AMEN

Leo J Vaillancourt